# The Library of the Nine Planets™

# EARTH

*Allison Stark Draper*

rosen central™

The Rosen Publishing Group, Inc., New York

*For my father*

Published in 2005 by The Rosen Publishing Group, Inc.
29 East 21st Street, New York, NY 10010

Copyright © 2005 by The Rosen Publishing Group, Inc.

First Edition

**Library of Congress Cataloging-in-Publication Data**

Draper, Allison Stark.
Earth/by Allison Draper.
    p. cm.—(The library of the nine planets)
Includes bibliographical references and index.
ISBN 1-4042-0167-X (library binding)
1. Earth—Juvenile literature. [1. Earth.]
I. Title. II. Series.
QB631.4.D73 2004
525—dc22
                                    2003023457

*Manufactured in the United States of America*

**On the cover:** A view of Earth taken from the space shuttle *Columbia*.

# Contents

Introduction                                      5

**ONE** Spaceship Earth                           7

**TWO** Birth and Life                            13

**THREE** The Face of Earth                       23

**FOUR** An Envelope of Air                       29

**FIVE** The Future of Our Planet                 34

Timeline of Exploration and Discovery            39

Glossary                                          40

For More Information                              42

For Further Reading                               44

Bibliography                                       45

Index                                              46

# INTRODUCTION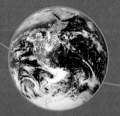

*Looking* up at the sky from a dark place on a moonless night, the visible stars and planets blend into a wash of light. If you could see far enough, the stars would form a solid wall of bright points in numbers that defy the human imagination.

Scientists think there are 10 billion galaxies in the universe. One of these is our own: the Milky Way. Appearing in the sky as a creamy oval smear, the Milky Way is composed of more than 100 billion stars and stretches 80,000 light-years across. A light-year is the distance light travels in one year, just less than 6 trillion miles (9.7 trillion kilometers). This means that a beam of light takes 80,000 years to travel from one end of the Milky Way to the other. The distance, therefore, is 80,000 light-years.

Two-thirds of the way from the center of the Milky Way to its edge, the density of the galaxy begins to thin. There, one star, 24 trillion miles (39 trillion km) from its nearest neighbor, is our Sun. It is surrounded by asteroids, meteorites, comets, moons, and nine planets. Earth, one of those nine, is the third planet from the Sun.

In space photography, next to gray Pluto, ringed Saturn, striped Jupiter, and red Mars, Earth looks lush and familiar. Its blue water glitters under swirling clouds. This water and the atmosphere that traps these clouds make Earth unique in the solar system.

Earth's atmosphere, or air layer, and its hydrosphere, or water layer, are protective envelopes around the planet. The atmosphere is the swirling blanket of gases, such as oxygen, that shields Earth from harsh radiation from the Sun and lets us breathe.

The hydrosphere includes all of Earth's oceans, lakes, streams, and underground waters and such water vapor in the atmosphere as clouds and rain. It provides water for plants and animals.

Earth's third protection layer is its molten core. This makes a magnetic field that protects us from the radiation from space. Together, these defenses are the reason Earth is the only planet in the solar system known to support life.

Earth is certainly a unique planet, not only for its lush environment, but also because it is the only one known to support life. But no one knows what further exploration will reveal about other planets. The Mars exploration rovers *Spirit* and *Opportunity* have searched for potential life on that planet. In March 2004, NASA announced the discovery of a new "planetoid" called Sedna, which orbits in the outer reaches of the solar system. Who knows what the future holds?

# Spaceship Earth

*For* the creatures that live on it, Earth seems like a self-contained spaceship that provides food, water, shelter, and heat. In fact, its ability to support us depends on its movement through space. If Earth were completely still, there would be no summer or winter, no day or night. Fortunately for us, the planet moves in two ways: It revolves around the Sun and it rotates.

Every 365.24 days, Earth completes a revolution (or orbit) around the Sun. Our calendar includes the extra quarter day by adding a full day to February every four years. This extra day makes every fourth year a leap year.

Since Earth's orbit is an ellipse, or oval, Earth is not always the same distance from the Sun. On January 3 of every year, Earth is only 91,650,000 miles (147,496,000 km) away, its closest point to the Sun, or its perihelion. It is at its farthest point, its aphelion, on July 4 of every year. At its aphelion, Earth is 94,760,000 miles (152,501,000 km) from the Sun.

Earth also rotates, or spins on its axis. Its spin changes its shape, making it bulge at the equator and flatten at the poles. At the equator, it is 7,927 miles (12,753 km) in diameter. This is 13 miles (21 km) greater than the distance from the North Pole to the South Pole. At the equator, Earth spins more than 1,500 feet (450 m) per second, which is almost 25,000 miles (40,000 km) per day. Toward the poles, where the circumference of the globe is smaller, Earth rotates more slowly.

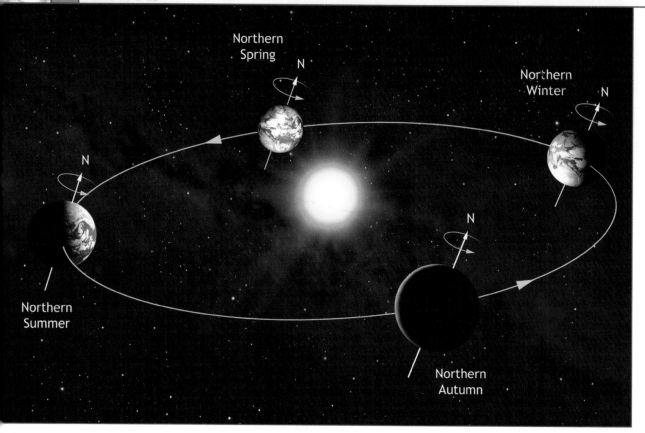

Depending on the tilt of Earth's axis, each hemisphere of the planet experiences a different season. In this computer diagram, the seasonal cycle of the Northern Hemisphere, which contains the United States, is shown. The Northern Hemisphere is pointed toward the Sun during summer. This allows the Sun's radiation to strike the hemisphere more directly, making that area of the planet warmer. In winter, the Northern Hemisphere is tilted away.

Earth spins on an imaginary axis between the North and South Poles. It turns to the east, which is why the Sun rises in the east and sets in the west. As Earth orbits the Sun, the tilt of Earth's axis changes. This creates the seasons, because at any one time only one hemisphere is pointed toward the Sun.

If you stand on the equator on March 21 of every year, the Sun would be directly overhead. This is the vernal equinox, or spring equinox. During the spring equinox, the days and nights are the same length all over Earth. The word "equinox" comes from the Latin words for "equal nights."

Three months later, on June 21 of every year, during the summer solstice, the Sun is directly over the Northern Hemisphere. This is the longest day of the year in the Northern Hemisphere. During the summer solstice, the North Pole has twenty-four hours of daylight, which means that there are no nights there.

On September 22 of every year, six months after the vernal equinox, is the autumnal equinox, which mirrors the vernal equinox exactly. As in the spring, the Sun is directly overhead at the equator. Days and nights are again the same length in both hemispheres. The winter solstice follows three months later, on December 21 of every year, when the tilt of Earth positions the Sun directly over the Southern Hemisphere. This is the longest day of the year in the Southern Hemisphere and the shortest in the Northern Hemisphere. There is no daylight at all at the North Pole.

## Earth Fact Sheet

**Diameter:** 7,927 miles (12,757 km)

**Mass:** 6,000,000,000,000,000,000,000,000 kilograms

**Average Distance from the Sun:** 92,955,820 miles (149,597, 890 million km)

**Length of Day:** 23 hours, 57 minutes

**Length of Year:** 365.24 days

**Number of Moons:** 1

**Average Temperature:** 59° Fahrenheit (15° Celsius)

**Atmospheric Composition:** 21 percent oxygen, 78 percent nitrogen, plus minor trace elements

# Earth's Ingredients

Stars create chemical elements, which are the building blocks for rocks and minerals. We currently know of 112 elements in the universe, 89 of which are found on Earth. The eight common elements that make up most of the rocks in Earth's crust are oxygen, silicon, iron, magnesium, aluminum, calcium, potassium, and sodium. The different amounts of elements in each create the immense variety of rocks on the planet. For example, granite and limestone have some of the same basic ingredients.

Many of the elements in the universe come from star explosions, or supernovas. Earth is made of particles from a star that exploded. Rare and violent, an exploding star glows more brightly than its entire galaxy. Then the remnants from the explosion scatter across the universe. About five billion years ago, some of the gas and dust from a supernova settled into a giant cloud. This is what some scientists call time zero, or the beginning of our solar system.

Scientists do not know exactly how the Sun and planets formed from the cloud. Possibly the middle became the Sun and the edges became the planets. Or all of the material may have clumped into the Sun with the planets forming around it. Over time, the Sun's motion may have spun off chunks of debris that formed into planets.

# The Unchanging Moon

The Moon is very different from Earth. It has no atmosphere and no exposed water, and it no longer has any volcanic activity. In fact, almost every rock on the Moon is older than every Earth rock. A 3.5-billion-year-old rock is very rare on Earth but very common on the Moon. This is because the rocks on Earth are constantly forming and breaking and reforming. On the Moon, nothing changes.

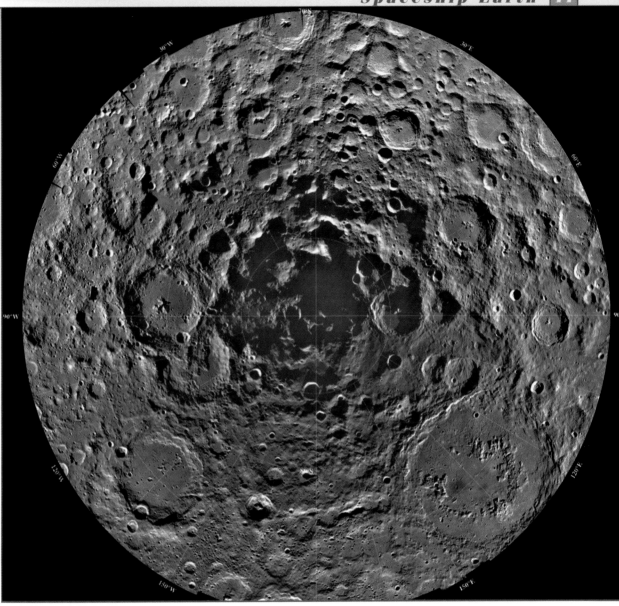

Since the Moon has no atmosphere to shield it from incoming objects, its surface is pitted with numerous craters. This image is a mosaic of 1,500 pictures taken by the satellite *Clementine* of the Moon's south pole. The shadowed area directly on the south pole indicates a major depression.

We used to believe there was no water at all on the Moon, but in 1994, the United States' satellite *Clementine* detected possible ice, or frozen water. If this was ice, it was probably deposited on the Moon by comets that collided with it. It has not evaporated because it lies in shadowed craters near the Moon's south pole.

Geologically, the Moon is simpler than Earth. Ninety-eight percent of its surface is made of only four minerals: plagioclase feldspar, olivine, pyroxene, and ilmenite. This surface is covered with a thick layer of ground-up rock fragments. A few feet down, this powder hardens into something like cement. Some of the Moon is composed of basalt, a dark, porous stone formed by cooling lava from the Moon's early volcanoes.

Looking at the Moon from Earth, even without a telescope, you can see that it is pitted with craters. Meteors made them. A clue to this is the breccias (rocks with signs of violent impact) all over the Moon's surface. Breccias on Earth are found only near meteorite craters. On the Moon, breccias are everywhere. Also, glassy pools of hardened rock at the bottom of many Moon craters are signs of the rapid cooling that follows the rock-melting heat of a meteorite impact.

# The Giant Impact Theory

For thousands of years, people have searched for an answer to the origin of the Moon. A clue may lie in the way the Moon spins around the Earth, like ice skaters holding hands. For Earth and the Moon, a violent blow from another object, roughly the mass of Mars, might have started this momentum.

The giant impact theory proposes that a mystery object crashed into Earth between 10 million and 100 million years after Earth was formed. The collision vaporized the other object and part of Earth. A vast cloud of debris shot into space. Some of it went into orbit around Earth. Its gases and dust cooled into solid rock. Over time, this rock formed the Moon.

Scientists will be able to take a closer look at the Moon in the future. On January 4, 2004, President George W. Bush proposed plans for astronauts to return to the Moon by 2020.

# Two

# Birth and Life

*Earth* is roughly 4.5 billion years old. The first 2 billion years of Earth's history are called the Precambrian era. Earth's oldest known rocks date from this era. They are 3.9 billion years old and were found in Canada. The fossils of some soft-bodied organisms also date back to this period.

At first, the planet was a ball of molten chemicals in a thin shell of stone. The shell cracked and melted continually. Solid crusts sank into the hot interior. Melted rock rose to the surface and cooled into new crust. All over the planet, volcanoes poured gases into the early atmosphere. The gases were a mixture of carbon dioxide and nitrogen, but there was no oxygen.

Some volcanoes grew so high that water condensed, or cooled into liquid, on their peaks because of the cool temperatures there. At first, these tiny drops evaporated as they hit the hot surface. As the crust cooled, they collected in pools that slowly grew into oceans.

Meanwhile, a light rock similar to granite rose under Earth's giant volcanoes. As the volcanoes eroded, these rock platforms became continents. This rock was very different from the rocky crust under the oceans. The ocean floors formed from komatiite, a hot, runny lava that reached temperatures of $3,100°F$ ($1,704°C$). This is twice as hot as any lava in the world today. As it traveled, the lava melted flattened trails of rock. In a week, a komatiite lava flow could cut a channel 65 feet (20 m) deep.

Earth was a violent place in its early years. This artist's rendition shows how the planet is believed to have looked 4 billion years ago. There were no trees, and rivers of komatiite flowed over the smoldering surface. The conditions were harsh and inhospitable, and no life is known to have existed. Life, of course, formed later, leaving open the possibility that life exists, or will someday exist, on other planets whose environments now resemble that of Earth's early years.

Without plants or roots to hold the rocks together, Earth's surface constantly weathered and eroded. Crumbling rocks spilled salty minerals into the water and made the oceans salty. The atmosphere over these new continents and oceans was rich in carbon dioxide and very heavy. At first, nothing could live in it.

## The Surge of Life

If the history of Earth were twenty-four hours long, the last 544 million years would take up less than four hours. Dinosaurs became extinct eighteen minutes ago, human ancestors appeared two minutes ago, and modern humans have existed for only two seconds.

## Earth's Geologic Timeline

- **PRECAMBRIAN ERA (4,500 to 544 million years ago)**

- **PALEOZOIC ERA (544 to 248 million years ago)**

  Cambrian period (544 to 505 million years ago)

  Ordovician period (505 to 440 million years ago)

  Silurian period (440 to 410 million years ago)

  Devonian period (410 to 360 million years ago)

  Carboniferous period (360 to 286 million years ago)

  Permian period (286 to 248 million years ago)

- **MEZOZOIC ERA (248 to 65 million years ago)**

  Triassic period (248 to 213 million years ago)

  Jurassic period (213 to 145 million years ago)

  Cretaceous period (145 to 65 million years ago)

- **CENOZOIC ERA (65 million years ago to present)**

  Tertiary period (65 to 1.8 million years ago)

  Quaternary period (1.8 million years ago to present)

    Pleistocene epoch (1.8 million to 8,000 years ago)

    Holocene epoch (8,000 years ago to present)

The earliest fossilized life forms are mats of blue-green algae called stromatolites. They are 3.6 billion years old. They date from the Precambrian era and thrived in Earth's early atmosphere of nitrogen and carbon dioxide.

At first, stromatolites were very successful. They blanketed the warm belt of Earth's equator with their thick mats. Their waste product was oxygen. Much of this oxygen burned up in chemical reactions, such as oxidation, or rusting. Some of the oxygen became the ozone that protects Earth from the Sun's ultraviolet rays. Over time, the oxygen began to build up in the atmosphere. It poisoned the stromatolites and made way for oxygen-breathing creatures.

Around 700 million years ago, life had developed so that animals breathed oxygen and emitted carbon dioxide and plants absorbed carbon dioxide and created oxygen. This period saw the evolution of the first invertebrates, or animals with no spinal column, including sea pens and jellyfish.

One hundred million years later, creatures with exoskeletons, or hard outer shells, evolved. These included the *Marrella*, which looked like a sea crab with a heart-shaped shell and jointed legs; the *Hallucigenia*, which had spines on one side of its tubular body and short tentacles on the other; the *Wixwaxia*, which looked like a worm with legs; and the *Anomalocaris*, which had a long flat body and fins on either side to help it swim.

Around 544 million years ago, in the Phanerozoic eon, life on Earth evolved rapidly. Many species from this time are the ancestors of creatures that still exist. In the Paleozoic era, trilobites crawled in the mud of the seafloors and graptolites swam in the oceans. The Cambrian period saw the emergence of chordates, or animals with nerve cords. The nerve cord is like a spine. Chordates are probably the ancestors of vertebrates, or creatures with spines.

This illustration shows the different stages in the evolution of humans. At left is the most primitive ancestor of humans, dating back 23 million to 15 million years ago. At the right is modern man. The different stages in between show man evolving into a species that began to walk upright and use fire and tools to survive. The inset image is a stromatolite fossil, dating from the Precambrian era. At more than 3 billion years old, it is among the oldest fossils ever found on Earth.

The Silurian period spawned land plants. The Devonian period gave birth to fish. Forests appeared in the Carboniferous period. A huge leap in animal size occurred during the Triassic, Jurassic and Cretaceous periods, when dinosaurs thundered over Earth. This was a fertile time. Flowering plants date from the Cretaceous period, which also saw an explosion in varieties of insects. Dragonflies and butterflies appeared and pollinated the flowering plants. Mammals similar to rats evolved. As recently as 3 million years ago, in the Pliocene epoch, the first human ancestors evolved. Modern humans, or *Homo sapiens*, emerged in the Pleistocene. We have existed for only 150,000 years.

# The Fossil Record

The record of all this life is preserved in rocks. Sometimes, the dead body of an animal or insect presses into the mud. This mud hardens into rock, saving the impression of the animal like a geologic photograph. This is called a fossil. Other fossils are actual animals. An insect trapped in sticky pine resin remains perfectly preserved as the resin hardens into amber. This insect retains not only its shape and appearance, but also its deoxyribonucleic acid (DNA), the building blocks for all life. Some amber insect fossils are 40 million years old.

This prehistoric insect trapped in amber is an example of a perfectly preserved fossil. During Earth's Jurassic period, insects would often find themselves in the path of resin that leaked from and ran down the trunks of trees. When the resin hardened into amber, it would imprison the insect. Protected from the environment, the insect's tissues remained fully intact for millions of years. Since they are so well preserved, insects fossilized in amber are among the most prized geological specimens.

Other substances, such as ice and tar, have preserved creatures, including humans, for tens or hundreds or thousands of years.

Earth's surface changes so fast that there is no place on the planet where geologic history lies buried in tidy, unchanged layers. To study Earth's past, geologists arrange rocks and fossils according to age. They look at how the animals in the fossils change over time. Sometimes they find matching rocks or fossils on distant continents, providing evidence that the continents were once joined. Fossils can also reveal strange information about other periods in the past, such as ice ages.

## The Snowball Earth Theory

Geologist Paul Hoffman believes complex life emerged after a catastrophe called snowball Earth, which occurred between 600 and 700 million years ago. The snowball Earth theory proposes that the oceans froze between the time of such single-celled creatures as algae and the birth of more complex creatures such as jellyfish and sea crabs. Most early life-forms died.

Temperatures dropped to an inhospitable -40°F (-40°C). Water could not melt or evaporate. There was no cloud cover and no wind. The snowball Earth remained this cold for 10 million years. Some microbes survived by clinging to deep-sea volcanoes, which were the only major heat source left.

Undersea volcanoes continued to release hot gases, which spilled through cracks in the ice and slowly warmed the bitter atmosphere. One of these gases was carbon dioxide. Today, carbon dioxide, a greenhouse gas, is part of the global warming problem because it traps heat. Like a greenhouse, it lets sunlight in but does not let heat escape. Seven hundred million years ago, after millions of years of being produced, the carbon dioxide finally trapped enough heat to melt the snowball.

Hoffman thinks the ice collapsed in just a few hundred years, in a maelstrom of floods and hurricanes. Temperatures rocketed to a blistering 104°F (40°C) and boiled the oceans. Chemicals fell in the form of acid rain and dissolved rock. There might have been several of these swings from snowball to boiling acid bath. When they ended 600 million years ago, complex life crawled out of the chaos.

# The Human Study of Earth

Scientists like Hoffman are always proposing new ideas. Some of them seem ridiculous now but will later seem obvious. Others will be disproved and forgotten. Current theories include Hoffman's snowball Earth theory, the giant impact theory, the theory of global expansion, and the theory of global warming. Some people believe global warming is the fault of humans. Others think global warming is the least of our worries because we will soon plunge into a devastating ice age.

## The Fall of the Dinosaurs

In the 1980s, Luis and Walter Alvarez theorized that 65 million years ago a huge meteorite struck Earth. This caused an ecological disaster that killed the dinosaurs. The Alvarezes based their theory on the fact that around the world there is a layer of iridium that dates from the last days of the dinosaurs. Iridium is a siderophile, or iron-loving element, and Earth's crust lacks other siderophiles. In contrast, primitive meteorites are full of them. It is possible that this layer of iridium is actually extraterrestrial material that the meteorite spread around Earth when it crashed.

Scientific theorizing, in an attempt to explain the world, dates from the beginning of human history. For instance, people did not always know that Earth is a round planet in space. Many early civilizations imagined that Earth was flat. During the sixth century BC, the Greek mathematician Pythagoras founded a philosophical school at Croton (now Crotone) in southern Italy. Known as the first pure mathematician, Pythagoras believed that everything in the cosmos could be described in terms of numbers. He and his followers studied math, music, and astronomy.

Some members of Pythagoras's school noticed how sailing ships vanished over the horizon as they sailed away from the shore. Sailors reported that different stars appeared in the sky as they voyaged far from home. These observations revealed that Earth was as round as an orange.

Using very primitive measurement tools, the followers of Pythagoras made quite a good estimate of the planet's size. Over time, by watching the stars, they realized that Earth was only one of many bodies in space, along with the Sun, the Moon, the stars, and the other planets.

In the third century BC, the Greek astronomer Aristarchus of Samos tried to figure out why the planets move from west to east, while the stars move from east to west. He suggested that Earth was not the center of the universe. Instead, it circled the Sun. For religious reasons, this was not a popular idea and was rejected for almost 2,000 years.

After the fall of Rome in the fourth century AD, the Greek curiosity about nature was replaced by an interest in the religious questions of Christianity. Scholarly works were written in Latin, and knowledge of Greek and Greek ideas faded. Until AD 1000, most educated Europeans believed the Earth was flat.

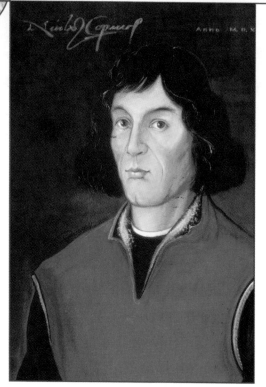

As a result of his revolutionary theory of a heliocentric solar system, Nicolaus Copernicus, shown here, paved the way for great scientific discovery. Later scientists such as Johannes Kepler, Galileo Galilei, and Isaac Newton all used Copernicus's theory as a basis for their own ideas, which furthered our understanding of Earth's place in the universe.

In 1522, the explorer Ferdinand Magellan circumnavigated, or sailed around, Earth. This proved that Earth was round. People were willing to accept this fact, but they objected when, in 1530, the Polish astronomer Nicolaus Copernicus, like Aristarchus, suggested Earth circled the Sun rather than the other way around.

Copernicus observed that Earth spins on its axis every day as it travels around the Sun once a year. These rotations create day and night. The tilt of Earth's axis creates the seasons of the year. The Catholic Church dismissed the idea that Earth was not the center of the universe. Copernicus's work was banned by the church until 1822.

Today, many ideas that were once seen as ridiculous, impossible, or blasphemous (in disagreement with religious ideas) are considered self-evident truths. It is hard to argue that Earth is not round when looking at pictures of Earth taken from space.

Ten or fifty or a hundred years from now, these ideas may prove to be one step toward a better understanding of Earth. No matter what happens with any one theory, it is important to continue to generate and encourage ideas. More than anything, we need to keep our minds open to the fact that in the incomprehensible vastness that is our universe, anything is possible.

# The Face of Earth

*Under* its continents and oceans, Earth is not a ball of solid rock. Twenty-five hundred miles (4,000 km) beneath the surface, there is a dense metal core with temperatures as high as 10,800°F (6,000°C).

No human or machine has ever been beneath the crust. Drilling into Earth is expensive and difficult. The deepest hole in the planet's surface is on the Kola Peninsula in Siberia, Russia, where the Russians have been drilling since 1970. This hole is now 7 miles (12 km) deep, which is only about half the thickness of Earth's crust. It has yielded some geologic information, but most of what we know about the interior of Earth we know from studying the surface.

In the 1600s, navigators noticed that the shape of the coasts of South America and Africa appeared to match. It looked like the continents had once been joined. In 1912, German scientist Alfred Wegener developed the theory of plate tectonics. This theory describes the surface of Earth as a group of large plates that slide around on molten rock. These rigid surface plates are called the lithosphere. The molten interior on which they move is called the asthenosphere. Moving 3 inches (7.5 cm) per year, the plates of the lithosphere slowly widen seas and build mountain ranges. Right now, the plate under India is pushing north into Asia and driving up the Himalayas, which are the highest mountains in the world.

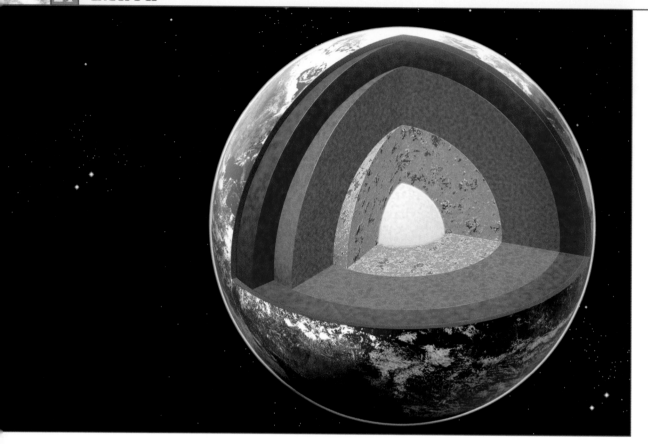

Earth is made up of several different layers, ranging from liquid metal to solid rock. This computer-generated diagram reveals Earth's various layers. The core at the center makes up about 15 percent of the planet's volume. The mantle—composed of the three layers surrounding the core—makes up about 80 percent. The remaining material exists in the crust, which is the outer layer.

Scientists study the interior of Earth using an instrument called a seismograph, which measures the vibrations that earthquakes send through Earth. The speed of these vibrations changes when the waves pass from rock to metal or from solid to liquid rock. By observing the changes in speed, scientists can determine the composition of the material that the waves are passing through. Early experiments with seismography showed that under the crust lie the mantle, the molten interior, and the core.

Earth's layers are composed of the following:

• The rocky crust, which is thicker under the continents and thinner under the oceans, or hydrosphere.

- The mantle, whose brittle upper section combines with the crust to form the lithosphere and whose lower section is the syrupy asthenosphere.

- The liquid outer core, made up of molten iron and nickel, which reaches temperatures of 10,000°F (5,500°C).

- The inner core, which is hotter and harder because the pressure at the center of Earth makes it solid. Temperatures are as high as 10,800°F (6,000°C).

Many scientists believe that the continents of today are all pieces that once formed a supercontinent called Pangea, shown here. Over millions of years, the pieces of Pangea drifted along the lithosphere to their present-day positions. According to the theory of plate tectonics, the continents continue to drift and may come together once again.

# Breaking and Building

The two major forces that keep Earth constantly changing are erosion and tectonism. Erosion wears Earth down from the outside. Tectonism lifts and fractures it from the inside. These forces work together to keep the surface of Earth in balance. Without tectonism, the weathering of erosion would wash North America into the sea in 25 million years. Without erosion, tectonism would make the whole planet look like the Himalayas.

Erosion includes rainwater that washes over cliffs, acids created by plants and lichens that eat into stone, sandy winds that scar mountainsides, and ice that cracks rocks apart. Running water is the most powerful erosive force. Every year, 100,000 cubic miles (160,000 cubic km) of moisture drop as rain, snow, sleet, hail, and dew. Two-thirds of this falls into the ocean. Ten million billion gallons (37 million billion liters) of water rolls across the land to the sea. Water creates streams and rivers, smooths stones, washes soil from fields, and carves underground caves.

The particles that the water carries scrape mountains and wear riverbeds. As a stream grows hard and fast enough to carry heavy rocks, it carves a wider path. Eventually, this riverbed grows so large that there is not enough water to fill it and the river slows. When it loses its force, the soil and plants it once tore out of its way start to grow back. The powerful river becomes a sluggish stream or even a swamp.

The Grand Canyon in the American Southwest is a spectacular example of the power of erosion. Carved by the Colorado River through layers of rock, the path of the canyon looks like a pair of facing staircases. It has been eroding for 10 million years. At points, the canyon cuts 6,000 feet (1,800 m) into the Colorado Plateau. The

The Grand Canyon, along with other canyons, provides valuable geologic information for scientists studying the history of Earth. Formed by the flow and continuous erosion of the Colorado River over millions of years, the canyon exposes layers of Earth difficult to see elsewhere. The layers serve as time capsules for the different periods over which the Earth formed.

river's destination, Lake Mead, is 2,000 feet lower (600 m), which means that the Colorado River will continue to dig deeper for another few million years. When it is finally level with the lake beneath it, the river will stop cutting forward and start cutting sideways, toppling the sides of the canyon. Eventually, the Grand Canyon will be a 50-mile-wide (80 km wide) floodplain between slanted bluffs. The Colorado River will be a lazy river in a bed thick with silt.

## The Theory of Global Expansion Tectonics

Plate tectonic theory, which states that the plates of the lithosphere move around the surface of the planet, changing the shapes of continents and oceans, is no longer controversial. Much of the world agrees that the continents once fit together like puzzle pieces. Since then, the plates on which the continents sit have spent millions of years drifting and colliding.

The theory of global expansion tectonics is more radical. It suggests that under pressure from the magma spewed by underground volcanoes, Earth's diameter has been growing continuously since its birth. This idea is based on the work of geologist Christopher Otto Hilgenberg, who observed that fitting all of the continents together, like pieces in a puzzle, would create a complete solid crust on a planet between 50 and 60 percent of the size of modern Earth. Earth expansionists believe that Earth's expansion, and not simple drifting, created the separations between the continents.

# An Envelope of Air

*Nonmarine* life on Earth inhabits the atmosphere the way fish inhabit the sea. Without the atmosphere, there would be no life. The atmosphere protects the planet and provides the rain that waters crops and erodes rock into fertile soil.

The atmosphere is made of gas. Most of the air is made up of nitrogen, oxygen, and carbon dioxide gases and water vapor. Oxygen is one-fifth of the gas in the atmosphere. People would not be able to breathe if there were less oxygen in the atmosphere. The atmosphere also contains dust and such human contributions as soot, car exhaust, and radioactive fallout particles from nuclear explosions.

## Sun and Storm

The atmosphere provides less protection for Earth where the angle of the Sun is more direct. At the equator, where the Sun is closest to Earth's surface, the atmosphere lets in much more radiation, or heat. This temperature difference creates movement in the atmosphere. Air warmed by the Sun rises. Heavy, cold air drops underneath it. This creates wind and weather patterns.

These patterns are complicated by the fact that Earth spins. If it did not, air would just loop between the poles and the equator. Instead, the air at different altitudes and latitudes drifts sideways. This creates the swirling or cyclonic form of storms.

Storms are formed by small eddies that blow around a center of low-pressure air. They spin counterclockwise in the Northern Hemisphere and clockwise in the Southern Hemisphere. This is like a miniature version of the motion of air in the atmosphere. The air at the center is lighter and lower in pressure. The heavier, higher-pressure air outside flows in toward the center.

In the opposite case, the eddy forms around a dense mass and the air flows out from the center. Spinning high-pressure formations sweep cold, dry air across the United States from northern Canada and bring cold, clear weather. These are fair-weather "highs."

## The Layers of the Atmosphere

- The troposphere is the layer that supports life. It is composed of 78 percent nitrogen, 21 percent oxygen, and small amounts of argon, carbon dioxide, other gases, and water vapor.

- The stratosphere begins 10 miles (16 km) above Earth's surface. There, ozone enters the mix. When electricity or strong ultraviolet rays pass through oxygen, they turn it into ozone. This layer absorbs most of the dangerous ultraviolet rays that the Sun sends toward Earth.

- The mesosphere starts 25 miles (40 km) above Earth and reaches up to 50 miles (80 km).

- The ionosphere is very thin but can reflect radio waves. This was how we sent long-distance radio signals around Earth before there were telecommunications satellites.

- The exosphere begins as a 900-mile-thick (1,500 km thick) layer of helium, which then turns into hydrogen. At 6,000 miles (10,000 km) from the surface of Earth, the exosphere ends and space begins.

Earth's atmosphere has various layers in which the air is composed of different chemicals. In this image taken by the International Space Station, the different layers are visible. They're distinguished by the colors red, orange and blue, with Earth at the bottom. At the top right is the crescent moon.

When two air patterns of different temperatures collide, they create a front. If a warm air mass replaces a cold one, it usually leads to heavy rain. When a cold air mass replaces a warm one, it may start as a line of dark clouds and grow into a violent thunderstorm or spin off the dangerous funnel-shaped vortex of a tornado.

## The Theory of Global Warming

Many scientists believe that humans are having a very negative effect on the weather. They say that burning fossil fuels such as coal and oil to heat homes or drive cars is raising temperatures around the world

Many scientists believe that the burning of fossil fuels by humans is pumping the atmosphere full of carbon dioxide and contributing to the greenhouse effect. The major types of pollution scientists believe contribute to global warming are the use of gasoline-consuming cars, the heating of our homes, and industry that gives off pollutants from manufacturing products.

by filling the atmosphere with carbon dioxide and other greenhouse gases. This rise in temperature is called global warming.

Not everyone agrees. Some researchers think that changes in the temperature of the Sun are more likely to heat or cool Earth than anything we could do. They also point out that the world has been warming up gradually for 20,000 years. Since the last ice age, the seas have risen because of the melting of the glaciers at the North and South Poles.

In 1990, the United Nations' Intergovernmental Panel on Climate Change predicted that Earth's temperatures will rise. Because this warming would change the balance of Earth's ecosystem, it could kill off certain plants and animals while increasing violent floods and storms. On the other hand, higher temperatures would make it easier to grow crops in cold countries.

The Earth's climate system is not very stable. On a geologic timeline, the window for human survival is narrow. A rise in temperature that would flood hundreds of miles of farmland or a mild ice age in which ice covered half of Canada would be devastating to the human population.

# Five

# The Future of Our Planet

*The* history of Earth is a study of geology, geography, hydrology, and biology. Its future is also a study of humans. People have joined the natural forces shaping Earth. A tidal wave may seem more destructive than forgetting to recycle, but Earth is a place of slow change, so everything counts. The Grand Canyon was not carved overnight.

As the human population grows, it consumes more. We use more land to build houses and farms, and we destroy more jungles and forests. This increases floods and landslides. Between 1970 and 2002, Earth's forests shrank by 12 percent. In the same period, partly because of overfishing, the variety of ocean life dropped by 33 percent. Freshwater ecosystems, traumatized by construction and pollution, declined by half.

If you measure a nation's consumption of grain, fish, wood, and freshwater, as well as carbon dioxide emissions from cars and industry, you can determine a country's "footprint" per person. This is the amount of land each person in a given country uses to stay alive.

In the United States, the footprint is 30.5 acres (12.3 hectares) per person. A western European's footprint is 15.6 acres (6.3 ha), an Ethiopian's is 5 acres (2 ha), and a Burundian's is 1.3 acres (0.5 ha). The nation of Burundi consumes the least resources per person of any country in the world.

Environmentalists believe we need to stop abusing Earth. This is good advice. A less stressed planet means a more secure home. Controlling nature is impossible. Violent

Many scientists believe that deforestation, the process by which forests are logged or burned, is slowly contributing to the greenhouse effect. This is because trees consume carbon dioxide. Without a healthy amount of trees, the carbon dioxide in our atmosphere increases, traps the Sun's radiation, and increases the temperature of the planet.

weather, volcanoes, and earthquakes are the workings of the living planet, not problems for humans to solve. On the other hand, it is foolish to cut down trees that keep farmland from collapsing into rivers. If we live on Earth as nondestructively as we can, the planet will continue to support and protect us for a long time to come.

## Surviving the Earth

Geologist Peter D. Ward and astronomer Donald Brownlee believe Earth is in the middle of a round trip. It will eventually return to a stage like its beginning. Its last creature may be a single-celled

Mars is one of the most barren and driest planets in our solar system. Some scientists believe that Earth may one day resemble Mars if its weather patterns continue to change. Shown here is the surface of Mars taken by the exploration rover *Opportunity*.

organism like algae in a stromatolite. Then the oceans will dry up and the atmosphere will blow away. Earth will be hot, oxygen free, and as barren as Mars.

Meanwhile, the Sun will continue to consume the hydrogen stored in its core, slowly growing into a cooler and much larger star. Billions of years from now, its expanding shell will engulf the planets one by one. Finally, the Sun will swallow and incinerate Earth.

This is a pretty grim vision. If humans last long enough to worry about it (so far we have lived only two seconds of Earth's twenty-four-hour life; dinosaurs lasted more than three minutes), we will need to figure out what to do next. Astrobiology, the study of the search for extraterrestrial life and the effects of extraterrestrial surroundings on living organisms, may provide some answers. According to Ward and Brownlee, "Astrobiology … [helps us predict] the kinds of planets that could harbor life."

Potentially, we might reach Mars, which is 50 percent farther from the Sun than Earth is. This would require us to "terraform" Mars, or to make its air, water, and soil like Earth's. It would also mean mastering space travel.

Going forward, scientists will continue to develop more and more theories to explain a world about which we understand only a

This artist's rendition of a proposed hydrobot, or underwater explorer, is shown beneath the ice of Jupiter's moon Europa searching for life. This device *(inset)*, called a cryobot, is designed to explore frozen lakes by melting ice and passing through it. In order to test these devices and others like it, scientists plan to send them to Lake Vostok, a subglacial lake in Antarctica, to replicate an extraterrestrial environment.

tiny fraction. We need to listen to them, question them, and do our own watching, thinking, and observing.

# Practicing for Astrobiology

Extraterrestrial research, or research of other planets, is expensive and dangerous. Fortunately, it may be possible to learn about the possibilities for life on other planets while staying on Earth. On August 11, 2003, NASA reported plans for work at Lake Vostok, 2.5 miles (4 km) beneath the eastern Antarctic ice sheet. Vostok has been sealed off from Earth's atmosphere since Antarctica became covered with ice more than 15 million years ago.

Scientists believe microorganisms live under Vostok's ice. They also think this sub-ice environment may be a lot like the one on Europa, one of Jupiter's moons. In the near future, international teams plan to tap into the water beneath Lake Vostok's ice sheet. What they find may help astrobiologists better understand the environment of Jupiter. It may even be a first step toward learning how to live outside of Earth.

**Circa 600 BC:** Pythagoras founds a school, which leads to the theory that Earth is round and to the first estimate of the planet's size.

**300 BC to AD 1000:** Educated Europeans cease to read the ancient Greeks and return to the belief that Earth is flat.

**1530:** Nicolaus Copernicus observes that Earth spins on its axis every day as it travels around the Sun once per year. This suggests, against the beliefs of the Catholic Church, that the Earth is not the center of the universe.

**1912:** German scientist Alfred Wegener develops the theory of plate tectonics.

**1969:** Neil Armstrong is the first man to walk on the Moon on July 20.

**1994:** The United States' satellite *Clementine* detects ice, or frozen water, on the Moon.

**2003:** On August 11, NASA announces plans for tests to be conducted on possible life-forms at Lake Vostok, Antarctica, to study the possibility for life on other planets

**Circa 300 BC:** Aristarchus of Samos theorizes that the Sun does not revolve around the Earth, but that the Earth revolves around the Sun.

**1522:** Ferdinand Magellan circumnavigates the globe, proving that Earth is round.

**1600s:** Explorers begin to notice that the shapes of South America and Africa appear to fit like a puzzle, introducing the theory that they were once connected.

**1822:** The Catholic Church officially lifts the ban from Nicolaus Copernicus's work, which proposed that Earth is not the center of the universe.

**1990:** The United Nations' Intergovernmental Panel on Climate Change predicts that Earth's average temperatures will rise and change the balance of the planet's ecosystem.

**2004:** On January 14, President George W. Bush proposes sending astronauts to the moon by 2020.

# Glossary

**aphelion** The point farthest from the Sun in Earth's orbit.

**asthenosphere** The lower layer of Earth's crust; the zone of Earth's mantle beneath the lithosphere that consists of several hundred kilometers of deformable rock.

**atmosphere** The envelope of oxygen and other gases around Earth.

**equinox** Either of the two times during the year when the Sun crosses the equator and days and nights are approximately equal in length.

**exosphere** The outermost layer of Earth's atmosphere, lying above the thermosphere and extending thousands of miles into space.

**fossil** A remnant of an organism that is preserved in Earth's crust.

**hydrosphere** The layer of water that surrounds the Earth, including the oceans, lakes, streams, underground water, and any water in the atmosphere.

**ionosphere** The outer region of Earth's atmosphere, which extends from a height of 25 miles (40 km) to 250 miles (400 km) above the surface.

**lithosphere** The outer part of Earth, consisting of the crust and the upper mantle, approximately 62 miles (100 km) thick.

**mesosphere** The portion of the atmosphere from about 20 to 50 miles (32 to 80 km) above Earth's surface.

**perihelion** The point nearest the Sun in Earth's orbit.

**seismograph** An instrument for measuring the intensity of movement in the Earth, especially those made by earthquakes.

**solstice** Either of the two times per year when the Sun is at its greatest distance from the equator.

**stratosphere** The region of the atmosphere above the troposphere and below the mesosphere.

**stromatolites** A mat or mound of microscopic blue-green algae, which is Earth's earliest fossilized life-form.

**supernova**  A rare occurrence in which most of the material in a star explodes and creates an extremely brilliant, short-lived object that emits vast amounts of energy.

**tectonic**  Relating to, causing, or resulting from structural deformation of Earth's crust.

**tectonism**  The process of deformation that forms such major features of Earth's crust as continents, mountains, ocean beds, folds, and faults.

**troposphere**  The lowest region of the atmosphere, from 4 to 11 miles (6.4 to 18 km) high, depending on latitude.

# For More Information

The American Museum of Natural History
Central Park West and 79th Street
New York, NY 10024
Web site: http://www.amnh.org

Dinosaur State Park
400 West Street
Rocky Hill, CT 06067
(860) 529-8423
Web site: http://dep.state.ct.us/stateparks/parks/dinosaur.htm

Grand Canyon National Park
P.O. Box 129
Grand Canyon, AZ 86023
(928) 638-7888
Web site: http://www.nps.gov/grca

The National Air and Space Museum
Sixth Street and Independence Avenue SW
Washington, DC  20560
(202) 357-2700
e-mail: info@si.edu
Web site: http://www.nasm.si.edu/museum

The Page Museum at the La Brea Tar Pits
5801 Wilshire Boulevard
Los Angeles, CA 90036
(323) 934-7243
Web site: http://www.tarpits.org

Woods Hole Oceanographic Institution
Information Office
Co-op Building, MS #16
Woods Hole, MA 02543
(508) 548-1400
Web site: http://www.whoi.edu

## Web Sites

Due to the changing nature of Internet links, the Rosen Publishing Group, Inc., has developed an online list of Web sites related to the subject of this book. This site is updated regularly. Please use this link to access the list:

http://www.rosenlinks.com/lnp/eart

# For Further Reading

Branley, Franklyn M. *Dinosaurs, Asteroids, and Superstars.* New York: Thomas Y. Crowell Junior Books, 1982.

Costa de Beauregard, Diane. Our *Planet Earth.* Monkato, MN: Creative Education, 2001.

Farndon, John. *How the Earth Works.* Pleasantville, NY: The Reader's Digest Association, 1992.

Gould, Stephen Jay. *Time's Arrow, Time's Cycle.* Cambridge, MA: Harvard University Press, 1987.

Gould, Stephen Jay. *Wonderful Life: The Burgess Shale and the Nature of History.* New York: W. W. Norton & Co., 2000.

Van Rose, Susanna. *The Earth Atlas.* New York: Dorling Kindersley, 1994.

Walker, Gabrielle. *Snowball Earth.* New York: Crown, 2003.

Weiner, Jonathan. *Planet Earth.* New York: Bantam, 1986.

# Bibliography

Asimov, Isaac. *The Ends of the Earth*. New York: Weybright and Talley, 1975.

Asimov, Isaac. *Exploring the Earth and the Cosmos*. New York: Crown, 1982.

Bailey, Ronald H. *Glacier*. Alexandria, VA: Time-Life Books, 1982.

Beiser, Arthur. *The Earth*. New York: Time-Life Books, 1970.

Branley, Franklyn M. *Dinosaurs, Asteroids, and Superstars*. New York: Thomas Y. Crowell Junior Books, 1982.

Chorlton, Windsor. *Ice Ages*. Alexandria, VA: Time-Life Books, 1983.

Costa de Beauregard, Diane. *Planet Earth*. Monkato, MN: Creative Education, 2001.

Farndon, John. *How the Earth Works*. Pleasantville, NY: The Reader's Digest Association, 1992.

Gould, Stephen Jay. *Time's Arrow, Time's Cycle*. Cambridge, MA: Harvard University Press, 1987.

Gould, Stephen Jay. *Wonderful Life: The Burgess Shale and the Nature of History*. New York: W. W. Norton & Co., 2000.

Lambert, David. *The Field Guide to Prehistoric Life*. New York: Facts on File, 1985.

Mackenzie, Dana. *The Big Splat*. Hoboken, NJ: John Wiley & Sons, 2003.

McPhee, John. *In Suspect Terrain*. New York: Farrar, Straus and Giroux, 1983.

Putnam, William C. *Geology*. New York: Oxford University Press, 1964.

Van Rose, Susanna. *The Earth Atlas*. New York: Dorling Kindersley, 1994.

Walker, Gabrielle. *Snowball Earth*. New York: Crown, 2003.

Ward, Peter D., and Donald Brownlee. *The Life and Death of Planet Earth*. New York: Henry Holt & Co., 2003

Weiner, Jonathan. *Planet Earth*. New York: Bantam, 1986.

# Index

## A

Alvarez, Luis and Walter, 20
*Anomalocaris*, 16
aphelion, 7
Aristarchus of Samos, 21, 22
asthenosphere, 23, 25
astrobiology, 36
autumnal equinox, 9

## B

breccias, 12
Brownlee, Donald, 35, 36
Bush, George W., 12

## C

Cambrian period, 15, 16
Carboniferous period, 15, 17
chordates, 16
*Clementine*, 11
continents, 13, 14, 19, 23, 28
Copernicus, Nicolaus, 22
Cretaceous period, 15, 17

## D

Devonian period, 17
dinosaurs, 14, 17, 20, 36

## E

Earth
    age/history of, 13–17
    atmosphere and hydrosphere of, 6, 13,
        24, 29–31
    composition of, 10,
    diameter of, 7, 28
    layers of, 6, 24–25
    life on, 14–17, 18–19, 19–20
    orbit and rotation of, 7–8
    seasons on, 8
erosion, 26
Europa, 38
exoskeletons, 16
extraterrestrial research, 37

## F

flowering plants, 17
fossils, 18–19

## G

geologic timeline, 15
giant impact theory, 12, 20
global expansion, 20, 28
global warming, 19, 20, 31–33
graptolites, 16

## H

*Hallucigenia*, 16
Hilgenberg, Christopher Otto, 28
Hoffman, Paul, 19, 20
humans/*Homo sapiens*, 14, 17, 19

## I

insects, 17, 18–19
invertebrates, 16

## J

Jupiter, 6, 38
Jurassic period, 15, 17

## K

komatiite, 13

## L

lithosphere, 23, 25, 28

## M

Magellan, Ferdinand, 22
mammals, 17
mantle, 24, 25
*Marrella*, 16
Mars, 6, 12, 36
Milky Way, 5
Moon, 10–12, 21

## O

ozone, 16, 30

# P

Paleozoic era, 15, 16
perihelion, 7
Phanerozoic eon, 16
plate tectonics, 23, 28
Pleistocene epoch, 15, 17
Pliocene epoch, 17
Precambrian era, 13, 16
Pythagoras, 21

# S

seismograph, 24
Silurian period, 15, 17
snowball Earth, 19–20
solar system, beginning of, 10–12
stromatolites, 16, 36
summer solstice, 9

Sun, 5, 6, 7, 8, 9, 10, 16, 21, 22, 29, 30, 32, 36
supernovas, 10

# T

tectonism, 26
Triassic period, 15, 17
trilobites, 16

# V

vernal/spring equinox, 8, 9
vertebrates, 16

# W

Ward, Peter D., 35, 36
Wegener, Alfred, 23
winter solstice, 9
*Wixwaxia*, 16

## About the Author

Allison Stark Draper has written books for young readers on science and history.

## Credits

Cover NASA; pp. 4–5 NASA/JSC; pp. 8, 25 © Mark Garlick/Science Photo Library/Photo Researchers, Inc.; p. 11 NASA/NSSDC; p. 14 © David Hardy/Science Photo Library/Photo Researchers, Inc.; p. 17 © David Gifford/Science Photo Library/Photo Researchers, Inc.; p. 17 (inset) Sinclair Stammers/Science Photo Library/Photo Researchers, Inc.; p. 18 © Vaughan Fleming/Science Photo Library/Photo Researchers, Inc.; p. 22 © Detlev Van Ravensway/Science Photo Library/Photo Researchers, Inc.; p. 24 © Roger Harris/Science Photo Library/Photo Researchers, Inc.; p. 27 © Michael K. Nichols/National Geographic/Getty Images, Inc.; p. 31 NASA/MSFC; p. 32 © Paul Hardy/Corbis; p. 35 © Luiz C. Marigo/Peter Arnold; p. 36 NASA/JPL/Cornell; p. 37 NASA/JPL/CalTech.

Designer: Thomas Forget; Editor: Nicholas Croce